W9-AJO-580

Antarctica

by Katie Bagley

Consultant:
Colleen Keen
Geography Department
Gustavus Adolphus College
St. Peter, Minnesota

Bridgestone Books
an imprint of Capstone Press
Mankato, Minnesota

Bridgestone Books are published by Capstone Press
151 Good Counsel Drive, P.O. Box 669, Mankato, Minnesota 56002
http://www.capstone-press.com

Library of Congress Cataloging-in-Publication Data
Bagley, Katie.
  Antarctica / by Katie Bagley.
     p. cm.—(Continents)
     Summary: Discusses the continent of Antarctica, including its landforms, regions,
ice shelves, plant and animal life, and the scientists who perform research there.
     Includes bibliographical references (p. 23) and index.
     ISBN 0-7368-1415-9 (hardcover)
      1. Antarctica—Juvenile literature. [1. Antarctica.] I. Title. II. Continents (Mankato,
Minn.)
G863 .B34 2003
919.8'9—dc21   2001007902

Editorial Credits
Erika Mikkelson, editor; Karen Risch, product planning editor; Linda Clavel, designer and
     illustrator; Image Select International, photo researchers

Photo Credits
Ann Ronan Picture Library, 22 (Roald Amundsen)
Colin McNulty/Outside Images/PictureQuest, 11
Digital Wisdom/Mountain High, cover
Galen Rowell/Corbis, 15, 22 (Mount Erebus)
Gamma/Robert R-Hubert A./PhotoNews, 9, 20, 21
ImageState, 17
PhotoDisc, Inc., 18, 19
Steve Pinfield/B&C Alexander, 22 (Vinson Massif)

1 2 3 4 5 6 07 06 05 04 03 02

Table of Contents

Fast Facts about Antarctica

Population: Between 1,000 and 4,000 people from many countries do research on Antarctica each year.

Highest point: Vinson Massif, 16,066 feet (4,897 meters) above sea level

Highest temperature ever recorded: 59 degrees Fahrenheit (15 degrees Celsius)

Lowest temperature ever recorded: minus 128.6 degrees Fahrenheit (minus 89.2 degrees Celsius)

Interesting facts: Ninety percent of the world's ice is located in Antarctica.

Antarctica is the driest and windiest continent in the world. Its average height above sea level is the highest of any continent in the world.

The South Pole is in Antarctica. Because Antarctica is located at the bottom of Earth, every direction from the South Pole points north.

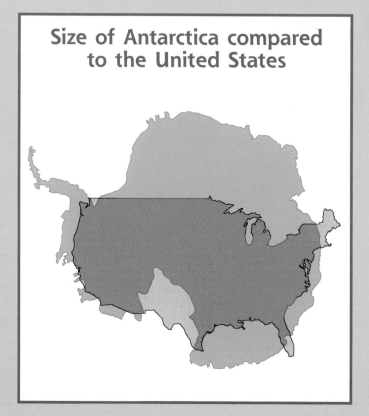

Size of Antarctica compared to the United States

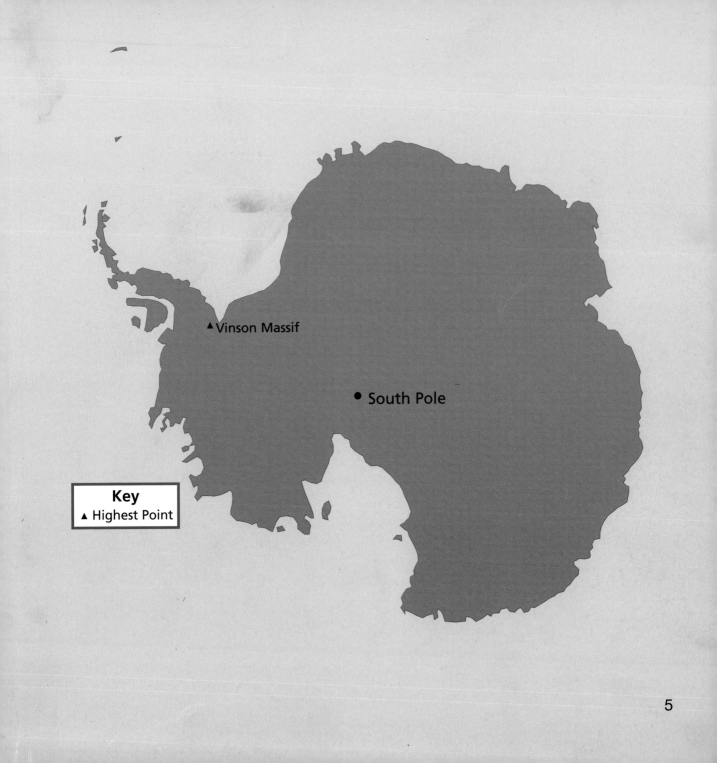

Vinson Massif

● South Pole

Key
▲ Highest Point

Antarctica

Antarctica is the fifth largest continent. It covers more area than the United States and Mexico combined. Antarctica is 600 miles (966 kilometers) south of South America. The Antarctic Ocean surrounds Antarctica.

ANTARCTIC OCEAN

Key

	Africa
	Antarctica
	Asia
	Australia
	Europe
	North America
	South America

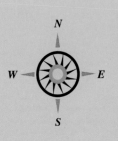

Antarctica's Land

Thick ice covers Antarctica. Snow does not melt there. Thin layers of snow build up over millions of years. The snow becomes ice. Ice in Antarctica can be up to 7,090 feet (2,161 meters) thick. The tops of mountains stick up through the ice.

Glaciers and Ice Shelves

Antarctica's ice slowly moves from the center of the continent out toward the coasts. The moving masses of ice are glaciers. Ice shelves form when glaciers move onto the water. Part of the ice floats on the water. Part of the ice remains connected to the land.

glacier
a large, slow-moving
mass of ice

Antarctica's Regions

Two regions make up Antarctica. East Antarctica lies in the Eastern Hemisphere. West Antarctica lies in the Western Hemisphere. Ronne Ice Shelf and Ross Ice Shelf are in West Antarctica. East Antarctica is colder than West Antarctica.

hemisphere
one half of Earth

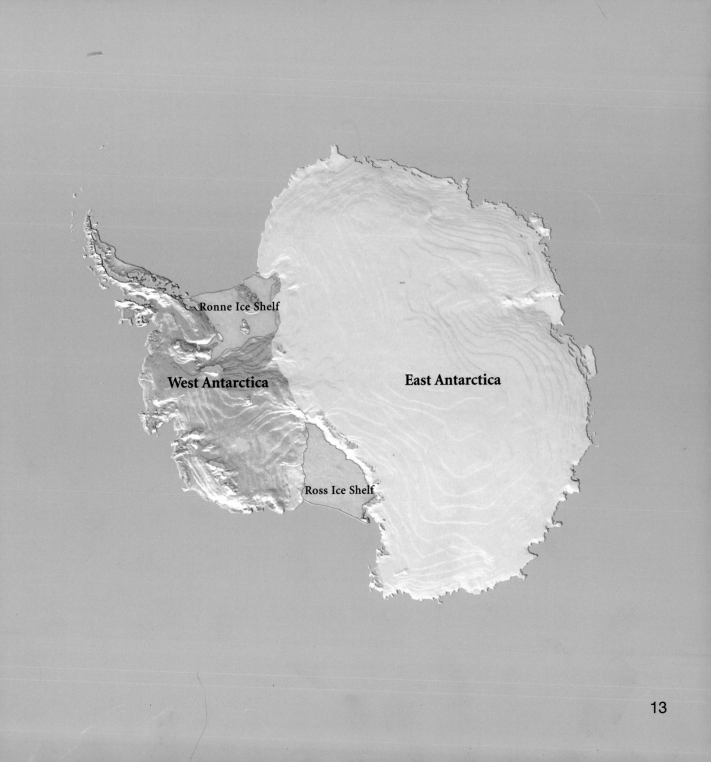

Ronne Ice Shelf

West Antarctica

East Antarctica

Ross Ice Shelf

13

West Antarctica

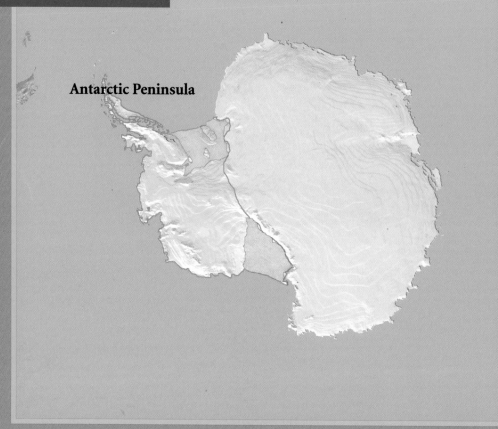

Antarctic Peninsula

Islands make up West Antarctica.

A single mass of ice covers all the islands.

Many volcanoes are in West Antarctica.

The Antarctic Peninsula is a chain of islands in West Antarctica. The peninsula sticks out toward South America.

peninsula
an area of land surrounded by water on three sides

East Antarctica is a large area of ice-covered rock. It rises from the ocean to a high plateau.

plateau
a raised area of flat land

The Transantarctic Mountains divide East Antarctica from West Antarctica.

Life on Antarctica

Antarctica's climate is harsh. The temperature almost never rises above freezing. Only tiny plants and insects live on Antarctica all year.

harsh
hard and unpleasant

Penguins and seals live on land during mating season. Whales and squid swim in the waters around Antarctica.

People are not native to Antarctica. Scientists from many countries go to Antarctica. They study the animals, plants, and atmosphere.

atmosphere
the mix of gases that surrounds Earth

About 1,000 people work in Antarctica during winter. In summer, about 4,000 people work there.

Reading Maps: Antarctica's Places of Interest

1. Vinson Massif is the highest point in Antarctica. Vinson Massif is 16,066 feet (4,897 meters) tall. Vinson Massif is on a part of Antarctica that has water on three sides. What is this landform called? Use the map on page 14 to answer the question.

2. The first explorer to reach the South Pole was Norway's Roald Amundsen. He traveled to the South Pole in 1911. Can you find another map in the book that shows where the South Pole is located?

3. Mount Erebus is a volcano. It is farther south than any other active volcano in the world. An active volcano is one that still erupts. Mount Erebus is in which region of Antarctica?

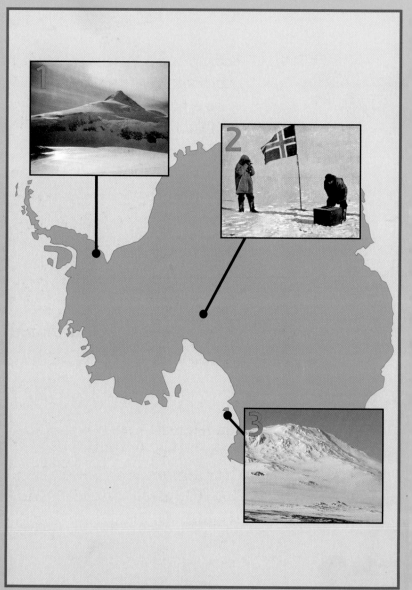

Words to Know

climate (KLEYE-mit)—the usual weather that occurs in a place; climate includes the average temperature and the amount of rain, snow, or wind.

continent (KON-tuh-nuhnt)—one of the seven main landmasses of Earth

native (NAY-tiv)—belonging to an area

plateau (plah-TOH)—a raised area of flat land

scientist (SYE-un-tist)—a person who does experiments

squid (SKWID)—a sea animal with a long, soft body and 10 fingerlike arms used to grasp food

region (REE-juhn)—a large area of land or water

volcano (vol-KAY-noh)—a mountain with vents; a vent is a passage that goes deep into Earth; melted rock, ash, and gases erupt through the vents.

Read More

Foster, Leila Merrell. *Antarctica.* Continents. Chicago: Heinemann Library, 2001.

Fowler, Allan. *Antarctica.* Rookie Read-About Geography. New York: Children's Press, 2001.

Petersen, David. *Antarctica.* A True Book. Chicago: Children's Press, 1998.

Internet Sites

Antarctica: The End of the Earth
http://www.pbs.org/wnet/nature/antarctica
Secrets of the Ice
http://www.secretsoftheice.org
Summer on Ice
http://www.csmonitor.com/atcsmonitor/specials/antarctica

Index